TWILIGHT

By Paul Breeze

*...a single act stage drama
written with mature actors in mind*

This play is available for licensing for amateur and professional stage productions and also for adaptation for radio, TV and film.

In the first instance, please contact the publishers by email at poshupnorth@googlemail.com or via the website at

www.poshupnorth.com

a single act drama written with mature actors in mind

First published in Great Britain in September 2012 by
Posh Up North Publishing
Nightingale Cottage, Reedley Hallows BB9 5JG

ISBN: 978-0-953978-21-2

British Library cataloguing in publication data.
A catalogue record for this book is available from the British Library

TWILIGHT

a single act drama written with mature actors in mind

LIST OF CHARACTERS

IVY
NELLIE
ADELE
STAN
RON
RENE

NEW MAN
EDITH POLECATE
FLORRIE

This play is dedicated to my own grandmother
Nellie Ann Whittington (née Robinson)
who was NEVER like any of these characters!

TWILIGHT

a single act drama written with mature actors in mind

SCENE 1

Three old ladies are sitting in armchairs in a bright and airy lounge. Two of them - IVY and NELLIE - are looking out of the window, the third – ADELE – has fallen asleep over her copy of "The Times".

IVY:	Looks cold out.
NELLIE:	Weather forecast said it would rain
IVY:	I haven't seen any umbrellas up yet
NELLIE:	There is a bit of a cloud over there though…
IVY:	Ooh look – there goes Iris – off to her coffee morning *(She looks at her watch)* She's late – it's almost 11 already.
NELLIE:	I always used to go to the coffee morning with Iris… till I had my stroke… she's always rushing around, that girl!

Off stage we hear a clock chime 11 times. IVY looks at her watch again and alters the time very slightly.

IVY:	Time for our coffee now then

IVY leans across and nudges ADELE

IVY:	Wake up Adele! Coffee time!

ADELE half stirs and then dozes off again. NELLIE looks up and acknowledges the arrival of a lady in a blue overall carrying a pot of coffee and cups on a tray.

NELLIE:	Lovely – I was about ready for this!

The assistant places the coffee, cups, milk jug and sugar bowl on the coffee table in front of the ladies and goes away again. IVY pours the coffee. She nudges ADELE to give her a cup.

ADELE:	I always have cream with my coffee! I can't drink it with milk…
IVY:	Well you've got this now haven't you…

TWILIGHT

NELLIE: You ought to call the servant girl back again and get it sorted out! How long have you lived here...? They ought to know by now! She always has cream in her coffee. Always has had, haven't you, dear!

IVY: You can't call them servants here, dear, oh no, they're carers. It's not really the same thing at all...

ADELE: *(as if still in a bit of a daze)* We used to have damned good servants as I recall...

IVY and NELLIE swap a "here we go again" type glance

IVY: Yes, anyway...

ADELE: Used to thrash 'em of course...if they stepped out of line

IVY: *(aside to NELLIE)* Singapore.... between the wars...

    (turns to ADELE) Yes, dear but times have changed now haven't they ...no more British Empire...just the European Community Market thing?

NELLIE: Got Ted Heath to blame for that haven't we...and that Attlee fellow – couldn't get out of India quick enough, could he..!

ADELE: Always had cream in coffee, lemon in tea and gallons of Singapore slings in the evening. Those were the days, I can tell you

NELLIE: Well, I think she ought to have cream if she wants it...After all, that's what these people are here for, isn't it...? I'll call her over... coo-ee Carol!

IVY: That's not Carol, she left to have the baby. What is that girl's name? Mavis..? Maggie, Millie..Maureen..?

NELLIE: No, it starts with an N – Norma, Nora...Susan..?

ADELE: Soo Ling! That's the name!

IVY: No I don't think that's it dear, I'm sure it starts with an M...

ADELE: Best parlour maid I ever had, I can tell you. Married a mango farmer and moved to Malaya

a single act drama written with mature actors in mind

NELLIE: Here, leave it to me, I'll get her for you.

NELLIE reaches down to the pedant alarm hanging around her neck and pushes the button. Off stage we hear an alarm sound and noises of people rushing.

NELLIE: Here she comes....now, dear, can Adele have some...
Ooh, where is she going?

There is a sound of doors slamming and feet rushing up some stairs.

CARER: *(off stage)* Room Five! Up the stairs!

NELLIE: Room Five? That's my room ...who's up there then?

IVY: They think you are dear. You pushed your pendant didn't you.

NELLIE: Well, I'm not am I? I'm here. No point going rushing up there if I'm down here is it? I could be having a heart attack and they'd run right past me on the way to somewhere I wasn't. Not very switched on, are they..?

SCENE 2

Three old ladies are sitting in armchairs in a bright and airy lounge again. IVY and NELLIE are looking out of the window. ADELE is engrossed in her "Times", doing the crossword.

IVY: Looks cold out.

NELLIE: Weather forecast said it wouldn't get above zero...

IVY: Too cold for snow though...

NELLIE: There's a heavy grey cloud over Will's Mother's...

IVY: Ooh look – there goes Iris – off to her Tai Chi session *(She looks at her watch)*

She'll be in good time any way, – it's not even 10 yet.

TWILIGHT

a single act drama written with mature actors in mind

NELLIE: It was me that first took Iris to that Tai Chi group... I heard about it first you know ... used to go every week, religiously ...till I had my stroke, of course... Iris! She's always rushing around, that girl!

IVY: Look – who's that coming up the path...? That man with the girl?

NELLIE: Not the doctor is it? Coming to see Maud?

IVY: Not the usual doctor, certainly. Perhaps he's a stand in. But, he's a bit old looking for doctor...they're all so young looking these days – like policemen!

ADELE: *(from behind newspaper)* And babies..!

IVY: *(ignoring ADELE)* Well, the girl doesn't look like a nurse so he can't be the doctor.

NELLIE: Look at that, she's just kissed him! Well, who'd have thought it - in broad daylight too! You'd think this was Holby City or Vets On Telly or something

IVY: Well, I don't think I'd like to be examined by a doctor who goes around kissing everybody. Oh no, you don't think he's **French**, do you?

NELLIE: That Dottie Patterson from church went to France to get her hip done – perhaps he's come to see her.

IVY: Yes but she doesn't live here though, does she?

NELLIE: Someone will have to tell him where to go.

IVY: Look, the head carer's gone and let him in. Perhaps he's come to see someone else.

NELLIE: Well, Rosemary needs her dressings changed but she's under Doctor Yorke.

IVY: Yes and Rosie won't take too kindly to being kissed, I can tell you. Cavey girls! He's coming this way...

A tall, well-dressed man of pensionable age comes on stage and addresses the ladies.

---

a single act drama written with mature actors in mind

NEW MAN:	Erm, excuse me ladies.... The head carer suggested I might like come and talk to you while she's finding her keys.
	My daughter's gone to look for somewhere to park...then we're going to have a look round.
IVY:	And who do you wish to examine exactly?
NEW MAN:	No-one. I've come to see the house, to look at the empty room.
IVY:	Well yes, in that case, you're very welcome. We were worried that you might have been one of those *"French doctors"*. Do sit down.
ADELE:	Who has the doctor come to see then?
IVY:	It's all right, he's not a doctor
ADELE:	What? Fancy coming in here, pretending to be a doctor! A girl's not safe in her own home any more. Somebody had better throw him out!
IVY:	Don't worry about her, doctor, she's a bit... well, you know...
NEW MAN:	Yes, but, really, I'm not a doctor
IVY:	But do sit down, please
NEW MAN:	Well, it shouldn't be too long now and I do a bit of trouble with my back....
NELLIE:	So, who has he come to see?
IVY:	He's come to look at the spare room, dear – he's a prospective resident.
NELLIE:	A doctor in the house! That'll be handy!
ADELE:	*(from behind newspaper)* What we really need is a plumber. My toilet cistern still doesn't fill properly.

TWILIGHT

a single act drama written with mature actors in mind

IVY: Well, we do need a few more men around here don't we...They've been a bit thin on the ground since Mr Johnson passed on.

ADELE: Oh yes! Now he **was** an expert with my plumbing!

IVY: He was an expert with everyone's plumbing, dear. That's probably what brought on his heart attack.

NELLIE: *(butting in)* Can you guess who's the oldest out of us..?

IVY: Oh not now Nellie, the poor man's just got here...

NELLIE: Go on, have a guess...

NEW MAN: Well.... I couldn't really....erm...

NELLIE: Ninety two...I am

IVY: *(whispers aside)* Act surprised!

NEW MAN: Oooh, are you..er... really? I'd never have thought...

NELLIE: Oh, yes oldest resident, me

NEW MAN: Well, that's erm,... isn't it!

NELLIE: Five years older than Elsie Blackmore and twice as fit...I could still do a Charleston. Shall I show you?

NELLIE makes as if to stand up but is pulled back into her chair by IVY.

IVY: Sit down you silly girl, you'll have one of your turns!

NEW MAN looks across the stage in the direction he came on and waves an acknowledgement

NEW MAN: Oh look – it looks as if the lady is ready to show me around – nice to have met you ladies!

NEW MAN hurries off stage.

IVY: Goodbye then, hope you like it here.
We could do with a few more men about the place....

ADELE: Has the plumber gone, then? He didn't look at my cistern.

TWILIGHT

---

a single act drama written with mature actors in mind

SCENE 3

IVY, NELLIE & ADELE are sitting in armchairs in a bright and airy lounge with their coffee on the table between them. IVY and NELLIE are looking out of the window. ADELE is engrossed in her "Times".

IVY:	Looks cold out.
NELLIE:	Weather forecast said it should be warmer today.
IVY:	Change the clocks soon don't we – when is it exactly?
NELLIE:	Middle of the night normally isn't it so it doesn't disrupt too many people.
IVY:	No, I meant which day is it we change?
NELLIE:	I forgot to do it one year. Didn't notice for three weeks. There was me thinking that they'd started putting the news on earlier!
IVY:	Started doing it in the First World War, apparently.
NELLIE:	What, to confuse the Germans?
IVY:	No, that was the roadsigns wasn't it.
NELLIE:	Was it?
IVY:	You remember, they took away the road signs so that if the Germans invaded, they'd get lost.
NELLIE:	Oh, yes. I remember that. My Ernie almost caught a spy once because of that.
IVY:	How do you mean, dear?
NELLIE:	Well, he was out in the road, mending our front fence and a man pulled up in a car and asked him the way to the next town.
	I'm not telling you that, my Ernie said, you might be a German spy. But I'm not a German spy, said the man. Well, said my Ernie, that's exactly what you **would** say if you **was** a German spy isn't it!

a single act drama written with mature actors in mind

	The next thing I knew, Ernie had got the man out the car and was waving a big screwdriver at him. He got me to go and fetch the constable… tell him we'd caught one of those Fiftominists…
IVY:	So then what happened?
NELLIE:	Oh, turned out he was the new regional manager for the Co-op…checking out his territory
IVY:	Well, what a relief!

IVY looks at her watch.

IVY:	So Iris will be almost there then.
NELLIE:	Where?
IVY:	Bournemouth.
NELLIE:	Bournemouth? Don't talk to me about Bournemouth! I went to Bournemouth way before Iris ever thought about going there!
IVY:	Yes, should she be almost there now. I saw her leave this morning early when her son came to pick her up.
NELLIE:	I thought she wanted to go abroad.
IVY:	Well she did at first. She was going to book one of those last minute deals to that "Thirty-Venturer" but then she found that her passport had run out.
NELLIE:	So what did she do then, then?
IVY:	Then she thought about going to Ireland.

ADELE rustles her newspaper furiously, then peeks over it, scowling first at the others, then at the audience. She turns back to IVY and NELLIE:

ADELE:	*(spits out)* Huh! Damned Fenians!

ADELE then goes back behind her paper just as briskly.
IVY gives ADELE a sideways look and then continues.

---

a single act drama written with mature actors in mind

IVY: As I was saying dear, before that... erm ..interruption...
                She was going to go to Ireland

ADELE: *(from behind newspaper)* Huh..!

IVY: *(ignoring ADELE)* but you need a passport to go there as
                well for some reason.

NELLIE: Oh, isn't it because Northern Ireland's part of the Euro or
                something...is that why that is?

IVY: No, that's the south, isn't it?

NELLIE: No, no, no, the south's a republic. Not part of the
                European Common Market....

IVY: So, anyway, she couldn't get her passport ready in time so
                her son has taken her to Bournemouth.

NELLIE looks up at the clock.

NELLIE: She must almost be there by now, then.

IVY: Do you think it's cold in Bournemouth?

SCENE 4

*ADELE, IVY & NELLIE are sitting in armchairs in a bright and airy lounge
again. IVY and NELLIE - are looking out of the window. ADELE is engrossed
in her "Times".*

IVY: Looks cold out.

NELLIE: Oughtn't be quite so bad today, so they say...

IVY: Not cold enough for snow then...

NELLIE: Well, it's quite bright overhead...

IVY: Ooh look – there goes Iris – out again!

NELLIE: Where does she go on a Tuesday then? It's a job to keep
                up with all her comings and goings.

TWILIGHT

a single act drama written with mature actors in mind

	Always in a rush that girl! Look at her nipping across the road like that. There's a crossing a bit further along.
IVY:	Flower arranging, I think – over at the Civic Hall. *(She looks at her watch and adjusts it slightly))*
NELLIE:	Huh! Don't talk to me about flower arranging! When I used to help organise the summer fete, I…
IVY:	*(interrupting)* Anyway, have you seen what's for lunch today? I shall be about ready for my lunch when it comes.
ADELE:	*(from behind her paper)* All that activity must be good for your appetite!
NELLIE:	Active? You talk about active? Before my stroke I was active. I am 92 you know….
IVY:	Yes we do know dear, you tell us every half an hour or so.
NELLIE:	So is it cold out then?
IVY:	Looks it.
NELLIE:	They said it wouldn't be so bad today.
ADELE:	Sausages
IVY:	(leaning across) Beg pardon, love?
ADELE:	*(peering over paper)* Sausages – for lunch – you asked what we were having.
NELLIE:	Well, I hope they take the skins off mine. I can never chew them properly.
IVY:	You should go and get your dentures fixed, like they told you at the clinic
NELLIE:	There's nothing wrong with my dentures and you know it. I've had them thirty two years and they were made by a skilled craftsman. Those NHS ones today don't compare.

TWILIGHT

---

a single act drama written with mature actors in mind

ADELE:	*(putting paper down)* Have you considered the possibility that your mouth may have changed shape over the past thirty-two years? And they may not fit properly any more?
	We're all on the downward slope you know…
IVY:	*(nodding)* Wouldn't get tuppence for the lot of us!
NELLIE:	Down ward slope nothing! There's nowt wrong with me. I'm 92 you know. Five years older than Elsie Blackmore and twice as fit…I could still do a Charleston…and a Blackbottom… if I had the right shoes, I could, any way.
ADELE:	"Raife" always liked his sausages.
NELLIE:	*(aside to audience)* That's her son. His name's Ralf but she always calls him "Raife" to show how cultured she is..
ADELE:	Had them every morning for breakfast on the boat out to India and insisted on having them ever since. We used to call them "snorkers". It was our little in-joke.
IVY:	So how is Raife then, Adele? I don't recall ever seeing him here.
NELLIE:	Huh, that's a sore point. Apparently, he doesn't come because she made her will over to some temperance charity
IVY:	Oh yes, that's right, he lives on a desert island with a native girl and drinks tequila all day long, or something
ADELE:	Hmmph, servants are servants and never the twain…

ADELE goes back to her paper

IVY:	That butcher on Cross Street always used to make good sausages. Do you remember, Nellie?
NELLIE:	That's right – Mr Townsend. Nice man. Won prizes for his sausages he did.
IVY:	Nice man. Retired after that business with the mad cows.

NELLIE nudges Ivy and speaks in a whisper, gesturing at ADELE.

TWILIGHT

a single act drama written with mature actors in mind

NELLIE:	Ere, do you think she's got it?
IVY:	Got what, dear?
NELLIE:	That mad cow disease..!
IVY:	Oh no, dear, she's just mad old cow. That's completely different.

SCENE 5

Two men are sitting at a dining table in a dining room. They are obviously not alone but the other diners are out of view.

ADELE:	*(heard from offstage)* Snorkers! Good – oh!
STAN:	Eee, that woman gets on mi nerves!
RON:	Who's that then, Stan?
STAN:	That Adele Gregory with all her airs and graces
RON:	Yeah, bit of a toff isn't she...
STAN:	You 're not wrong there, lad, not wrong at all.
RON:	Goes on about servants and the Raj as if we were still in the 1930s
STAN:	She probably thinks we are...
RON:	Sausages today then
STAN:	Good old bangers and mash

Carer comes and places plates on the table in front of the men.

RON:	Well, they may be bangers but that's certainly not mash
STAN:	Looks more like chips
RON:	All right, sausage and chips then, that'll do me

a single act drama written with mature actors in mind

STAN:
No egg and beans though… can't be sausage and chips can it – what was the menu for today supposed to be then?

RON:
Leave it to me Stan, I'll sort this out once and for all.

RON stands up and walks across the room to where the week's menu is hanging on the wall. He peers at it closely and then comes back to his table.

RON:
Hey! Do you know, Stan. it's not sausages and chips or sausages and mash.

STAN:
It doesn't surprise me at all Ron, that doesn't. They're always mucking about with the menu. Last week we were supposed to be having lamb stew and mash, and they ended up serving some fiddly "ragu", so they called it.

RON:
I blame that new chef – classically trained at some flash restaurant in London apparently. Mo-rees his name is. Takes perfectly good food and mucks about with. Do you remember, he took "sandwiches with your choice of filling" and replaced it with "sandwich oh choiks". I can't stand fish in bread!

STAN:
Me neither. Anyway what is it today then?

RON:
According to the menu, it's "sorsis and frights".

STAN:
More French muck! I tell you it was a lot better when old Mrs Wicks used to do all the cooking. Her steak and kidney puddings were legendary!

RON:
Still, we are supposed to be being more continental, aren't we – more tolerant of other Europeans so I suppose that means eating their erotic foodstuffs.

STAN
I think you mean exotic, Ron

RON:
You wot, Stan?

STAN:
It's exotic, the food, not erotic. Erotic's them dancers that they used to have on at the Working Men's on a Sunday lunchtime

RON:
I know what I mean – I was in the Navy! Nudge nudge..

TWILIGHT

a single act drama written with mature actors in mind

The pair start to poke at the food on their plates. Ron picks up a sausage on his fork

STAN: Well, it's a long time until tea... Could always give it a try I suppose...

STAN hesitantly takes a mouthful of food and then starts munching appreciatively

STAN: Mmmm…

RON begrudgingly does the same

RON: Tastes like sausage and chips to me….

STAN: Forgotten the peas though, haven't they…

SCENE 6

ADELE, IVY & NELLIE are sitting in armchairs in a bright and airy lounge again. IVY and NELLIE - are looking out of the window. ADELE is engrossed in her "Times".

IVY: Looks cold out.

NELLIE: Maud said it was bitter cold first thing when she went for her hair

IVY: Don't think it'll snow though…

      Ooh look – there goes Iris – out again! What is it today?

NELLIE: What day is it today? I lose track.
      She's always rushing somewhere, she is!

IVY: Look out – here comes Edith Polecat! I wonder what she wants this morning. Come to do some poor soul another good turn I expect.

NELLIE: Oh no! It's Wednesday – the first Wednesday in the month!

IVY: What's so special about the first Wednesday in the month?

TWILIGHT

a single act drama written with mature actors in mind

NELLIE: It's the bingo morning at the church hall. That'll be where Iris has gone. Pretend I'm asleep!

NELLIE lays her head on her shoulder and makes simulated snoring noises.

IVY: Nellie! What's happening? Are you ill? Why are you making that noise?

NELLIE: Look, when Edith Polecat comes, just tell her I'm asleep. Say I've been a bit under the weather and shouldn't be disturbed.

IVY: Why's that then Nellie?

NELLIE: She wants to take me to the bingo – show everyone she's doing her civic duty for the poor OAPs…

IVY: Well, that'll be nice, won't it?

NELLIE: Huh! She doesn't do it for **us** she does it for **her.** The last time she pushed me around in that frightful wheelchair and made condescending comments about how nice it was for me to get out a bit… anyway, it's full of OLD people!

IVY: Oh dear

NELLIE: And she hardly spoke to me the whole time. Too busy telling everyone how much she does for the "poor old folk…". If I hear her call me dear again in that tone I'm sure I will scream! Look out, here she comes! …remember what to say!

NELLIE puts her head down again makes more snoring noises.

An overly dressed lady sweeps onto the stage as if expecting applause and addresses the ladies in a very put-on condescending voice.

EDITH: Good morning ladies, how absolutely *lovely* to see you all again!

IVY: Is it, oh dear…

ADELE: (*from behind paper*) Huh! Polecat!

EDITH: Do you know, I've just has the most TERRIBLE news from the kitchen

TWILIGHT

a single act drama written with mature actors in mind

IVY: Oh really, dear what's that?

EDITH: No lemon dear! No lemon for my tea! Have you ever heard
                of another so awful?

ADELE: (*from behind paper*) Huh! How awful for you!

EDITH: (*Ignores her*) Come on Nellie, dear, we're supposed to be
                going to the bingo.

NELLIE doesn't move and continues to make snoring noises.

EDITH: Oh, she's dropped off…the little love, bless her!
                Come on, dear, time for the bingo! Look I'll get your coat.

*EDITH turns her back on the ladies to fetch a coat from a coat rack right of
stage. As she does so, NELLIE swings at her with her walking stick. IVY just
stops her in time.*

IVY: Calm down, dear. No need for that

NELLIE: I told you I'd flip if she called me "dear" in that silly voice.

IVY: Look out! She's coming back!

NELLIE: You tell her what I told you.

NELLIE goes back to her snoring noises. EDITH returns to centre stage.

EDITH: Has she sill not woken up? Should I get someone to
                come?

ADELE: Getting **someone** to GO would be better!

IVY: Well, she's just a bit under the weather at the moment.
                Needs plenty of rest – not too much excitement, you know
                how it is at that age…poor dear!

NELLIE: (*hissing*) Don't you start as well!

IVY: (*aside*) Hush, I'm just playing along with her

EDITH: Well, I really don't want to make her any worse, poor dear!

TWILIGHT

a single act drama written with mature actors in mind

NELLIE restrains a stifled growl

IVY: Best leave it to another time, eh?

EDITH: Well, I could take someone else. The car's just outside and I've put the wheelchair in and everything.

IVY: Yes, I'm sure you'll find someone else to take.

EDITH: Well, I'm not sure. I get the feeling that people here don't really like me...sob, sob

ADELE: Can't think why!

IVY: Of course we like you...we all like you! All the things you come and do out of the goodness of your heart for poor little us! Carpet bowls... charades...chocolate bingo...*(becoming more sarcastic)* – chocolate teapot more like...!

NELLIE: *(without raising her head)* Oh god! Do stop it!

EDITH moves closer to IVY and crouches down in front her.

EDITH: Do **you** like me?

IVY: Of course I do dear...everyone does.

EDITH: Perhaps I could take you to the bingo instead

IVY: Of course... what? Me? Oh, I er....

EDITH: Perfect! I'll get your coat! You can walk to the car, I'll help you

EDITH bounds off and gets another coat from the rack.

NELLIE: Ha, now you've done it.

IVY: But I was only...

EDITH comes back with the coat and yanks IVY to her feet.

IVY: But I was only....

EDITH leads a reluctant IVY off stage, talking all the way.

TWILIGHT

a single act drama written with mature actors in mind

IVY: But I was only....

EDITH: Come on then, dear, we'll have a lovely trip out in the fresh air. Think how nice it will be for you to get out for a while. We can look at the flowers in the new flowerbed.... Won't that be LOVELY...!

IVY: Is it cold out, dear?

As EDITH and IVY leave, ADELE lowers her paper to watch them pass. Once they have left the stage, she gives NELLIE a nudge and motions in the direction of the departed pair.

NELLIE sits up straight and gives a little cheer of celebration. NELLIE and ADELE share a knowing nod and ADELE goes back to behind her paper.

NELLIE: Well, it **will** be nice for Ivy to get out for a bit...

ADELE: Huh! Polecat!

SCENE 7

7 chairs are set out in a semi circle facing towards the TV, which is front of stage. IVY, NELLIE and ADELE are in the centre with one vacant seat between them. ADELE is reading her TIMES. STAN and RON are to the extreme left. The chair to the extreme right is also empty.

IVY: Gets dark early these days doesn't it....

NELLIE: Soon be spring, then we put the clocks back

IVY: Haven't had one of these video evenings for a while, have we...?

RON: Waste of time if you ask me...

NELLIE: What's the film then?

RON: It'll be some old black and white thing with Leslie Howard in it, I'm telling you. Once you get past a certain age, they think you only like black and white... I'd rather be up in my own room watching Coronation Street...

TWILIGHT

a single act drama written with mature actors in mind

NELLIE: Ooh, what time's that on? I like that!

IVY: Well, they ARE making an effort aren't they…trying to put on things for us to do …. we ought to give it our support

RON: Never actually ask us what we'd like to do, do they?

IVY: Well, they are **volunteers**, aren't they dear...

RON: Yes that's as may be. But just because you pass 70, it doesn't mean that you suddenly become interested in whist drives and carpet bowls does it?

ADELE: Never put on any male strippers, do they…

IVY: But they do volunteer their time don't they… for our benefit. So I suppose that we ought to try and appear grateful..

RON: Yes, but who in their right mind would want to watch some grainy old film from 60 years ago when you can go down the video shop and get out whatever you want for a couple of quid any night of the week …daft!

NELLIE: I used to like Leslie Howard … I cried when he got killed

Another resident comes into the lounge and everybody falls silent. They nudge each other, swap glances and start taking about the woman.

NELLIE: Who's that then?

IVY: Oh! You know who that is… that's the new arrival … Mrs erm…. Mrs erm...

ADELE: Phillips… Rene Philips…

IVY: That's it, Mrs Phillips

NELLIE: But where's she going to sit?

STAN: Look she's going to Mrs Rowland's seat…

RENE walks across the stage and motions towards the empty chair on the far side.

RENE: Mind if I sit here?

TWILIGHT

a single act drama written with mature actors in mind

Everybody looks at the floor and says nothing. STAN gets up and leaves the stage. RENE sits down and gets ready for the film.

NELLIE: (*whispers loudly*) That's Mrs Rowland's seat – she can't sit there…someone better tell her…

IVY: Oh dear, what should we do?

ADELE: You'd better tell her… she won't know otherwise.

IVY plucks up the courage and leans across to address RENE

IVY: Erm, excuse me dear… that's Mrs Rowland's seat. She always sits there.

RENE: Oh, I am sorry, I didn't know. Is she coming down for the video, then?

ADELE: She's in hospital.

RENE: Hospital?

IVY: Yes she's having her leg done – operation's tomorrow, I think.

RENE: So why can't I sit here then? If she's not coming to watch the film?

IVY: Well, it's her chair isn't it. She's be upset if she knew anyone else was sitting in it.

NELLIE: I get it once she's gone though. She said I could. I'm 96 you know…

IVY: You're 92 dear…

RENE: Well, I don't want to upset her, do I? I'll move.

RENE goes to stand up.

RENE: I'll sit next to you in the middle there shall I?

NELLIE: Oh no, she can't sit there.

ADELE: No, you can't sit there – that's Monica James' seat.

TWILIGHT

---

a single act drama written with mature actors in mind

RENE: Is she coming down for the film then?

Silence and fidgeting.

RENE: Is she in hospital as well?

More silence and fidgeting until IVY eventually leans over and whispers in a confidential manner

IVY: She's moved on…you know…to the **next place**

RENE: Oh, I'm sorry…

Knowing nods all round

IVY: Yes, we were all rather shocked – it was quite sudden

RENE: You must miss her

IVY: Oh we all do, poor Monica, she was so bright and cheerful. Adele was closest to her.

RENE: You poor dear, I am sorry. You must miss her terribly..

ADELE: Oh, I still speak to her…

RENE: Yes, I'm sure you do dear…

ADELE: Oh I do, quite often in fact.

RENE: Yes, whatever helps you feel better dear…(*aside*) different people grieve in different ways, don't they

ADELE: I see her too

RENE: Do you? Have you spoken to anyone about this? A counsellor, perhaps?

IVY: My oldest son's on the council – Park Ward, I think it is

ADELE I told Nellie, didn't I Nellie? You saw her too, didn't you?

NELLIE: That's right we had a coffee together…

RENE feels rather unnerved at this and stands up

a single act drama written with mature actors in mind

RENE: Had a coffee with her? Oh no…they must all be suffering from group hysteria! Unable to cope with the death of a fellow resident. I can't stand this…I'm off to watch Coronation Street.

RENE walks off in the direction she came.

ADELE: Strange girl! Fancy getting in a paddy like that!

NELLIE: All over a coffee!

IVY: Perhaps she doesn't know they have coffee mornings up at the intensive nursing home. Are you going tomorrow, dear?

ADELE: Oh yes, I've got to fetch Monica some books more from the library. She's done nothing but read since they moved her in there.

STAN reappears with an extra chair

STAN: Doesn't she want a chair then?

SCENE 8

IVY & NELLIE are sitting in armchairs in the lounge again. IVY and NELLIE - are looking out of the window. The chair that ADELE usually occupies is empty.

IVY: Looks cold out.

NELLIE: Yes, I saw a lady with a fur hat on earlier.

IVY: Think it might snow, then?…

NELLIE: Sky looks too clear to me.

IVY: Shame about Adele, wasn't it?

NELLIE: Well, at least it was quick wasn't it. Better she didn't suffer.

IVY: Just hope we can all go like that really

a single act drama written with mature actors in mind

NELLIE: Well, she had a good life didn't she

IVY: Oh yes, she had a good life... a good life...

NELLIE: I suppose they'll be having someone new in her room now the funeral's over.

IVY: Did you go, dear?

NELLIE: Go where, dear?

IVY: To the funeral..

NELLIE: You know I didn't. It was yesterday morning. I sat here and had coffee with you, didn't I?

IVY: Oh yes, so you did... silly me.

NELLIE: Anyway, you can't keep going to funerals every time somebody dies, can you...? I never have room for my tea afterwards...

               Did you go?

IVY: Ooh, now you're asking.... I can't remember ... when was it, again?

               Look here comes Rene – she went.

RENE arrives on stage and sits down in ADELE's empty chair. She moves the newspaper and puts it on the coffee table. This seems to annoy IVY and NELLIE.

NELLIE: Huh – she's only been gone five minutes!

RENE: Alright if I sit here and keep you girls company for a while until coffee time?

IVY: Yes, of course. You went to the Adele's funeral didn't you.?

RENE: That's right. I didn't really know her that well but I thought, with so few people from here going, I ought to go and show willing.

TWILIGHT

a single act drama written with mature actors in mind

IVY:	Did I go?
NELLIE:	Course you didn't dear! We sat here and had coffee like we always do. Don't you remember?
RENE:	I'm surprised more people didn't go from here.
IVY:	Oh, we don't go to funerals as a rule…
RENE:	Why's that then?
NELLIE:	Worried they might bury the wrong one I suppose…
IVY:	Let's just say they come round a little too often and they're never much fun…
NELLIE:	Anyway, you can't keep going to funerals every time somebody dies, can you…? I never have room for my tea afterwards…
	I'm with the Co-op. Was she with the Co-op?
IVY:	Oh no dear, Adele was with Mrs Lewis's. The upmarket one, you know.
NELLIE:	Oh yes, that's right, she does special options in the upholstery and things doesn't she.
IVY:	Adele always said she didn't want to be buried like any old body. She wanted her last journey to be in the utmost comfort.
	She had the "Imperial Connoisseur Package". Egyptian cotton, Belgian lace, special music - planned it to the last detail months ago. Prepaid and everything.
NELLIE:	They've got a "cremation club" at the Co-op, you know. I pay a fiver a week and regardless of what you've paid in, they do the same service.
	My Ernie had a great laugh about it before he went. Made up for dying young, he said – getting a top notch funeral for 20 quid!

a single act drama written with mature actors in mind

RENE: *(looking rather uncomfortable)* Hmm, very interesting. Well, I'd better not keep you – I've just remembered I left the peas on

RENE gets up and hurries away

NELLIE: Oh, look. Who's that coming up the path?

IVY: New cleaner perhaps? She looks very downtrodden.

NELLIE: Can't be a cleaner, she's coming in the main entrance. Oh no, the manager woman is sending her over here.

A very down at heel and humble looking lady of about 70 comes over to the ladies

FLORRIE: Excuse me ladies, could I came and talk with you for while? The manageress said that you were friendly with my cousin.

IVY: Your cousin? Who's your cousin? Is she a cleaner here?

FLORRIE: No, not a cleaner, not at all, she was a resident here... Ada? I believe she used to sit and have coffee with you here.

NELLIE: Ada? Ada? Who's she on about? You mean Adele surely. Read the "Times"... had cream in her coffee...

FLORRIE: Yes that must be her

IVY: Oh....Adele's family... come to finish emptying her room have you? Her friend Joan has done most of it already...

FLORRIE cautiously sits in the vacant chair and looks uncomfortable.

NELLIE: That son of hers didn't come.... Didn't even turn up for the funeral, I believe.

IVY: Yes, Mrs Bescott was most put out....

NELLIE looks at IVY in puzzlement, then looks out at the audience

NELLIE: *(whispers aside)* Who's Mrs Bescott?

FLORRIE: What little Tommy? Well, he wouldn't have, would he...?

a single act drama written with mature actors in mind

IVY: No, not Tommy, what's his name Rolf? Ralf? Raiphe? That one in India, anyway..

FLORRIE: Oh no, Ada, I mean Adele... only ever had the one son. She couldn't have any more after the operation...

IVY: So why has this Tommy never come to see her then? Ralph, I can understand if he's out in the colonies somewhere...

NELLIE: Hey! Guess who's the oldest out of us!

IVY: Oh don't start that again... I want to know about this Tommy boy.

FLORRIE: Well little Tommy was killed in the bombing. Didn't she say?

NELLIE: The bombing? Singapore? Hong Kong?

FLORRIE: Salford.

IVY: Salford? What ever was she doing in Salford?

FLORRIE: Our Ada worked in an armaments factory during the war. Didn't she say?

NELLIE: Oh no, that's all wrong... she was in Singapore then India, had snorkers on the boat and slings in the bar... she told us

IVY: At least that's what she *told* us...

FLORRIE: She may have told you that but I can assure you that she spent the war years working in a factory in Salford. She had a son called Tommy who was killed in the blitz and never had no son called Rolf.

  Her husband Jack....

IVY: Not Clifford...?

FLORRIE: Her husband JACK was killed in North Africa in 1941. Then little Tommy was killed when the digs they lodged in were bombed in 1942.

a single act drama written with mature actors in mind

	After the war I never saw her again. She went off an *"reinvented herself",* as I believe the modern term now is. Her solicitor just contacted me recently to tell me she had died and that I was her only living relative
IVY:	Oh, poor Ralph!
NELLIE:	So she never went to Singapore then?
FLORRIE:	Never even went so far as France so far as I know
NELLIE:	Never had servants?
FLORRIE:	Lived on her own as a recluse until she came here apparently... Had a win on the pools and decided to have a bit of comfort in her last years...
NELLIE:	To think! She had us all rushing round getting special cream for her coffee and biscuits from Fortnum's and ...
IVY:	Well, I always said she was a mad old cow....

Silence for a few moments

IVY:	Is it cold out, love? ... looks it...

THE END

Also available from the same author:

ISBN:
978-0953978281

146 pages
paperback

Available via Amazon, Kindle, Posh Up North Publishing and all other quality outlets....